THE MIRROR

THE MIRROR

INNER REFLECTIONS

MITRA

PARTRIDGE
A Penguin Random House Company

To order additional copies of this book, contact
Partridge India
000 800 10062 62
orders.india@partridgepublishing.com

www.partridgepublishing.com/india

CONTENTS

Dedication

Dedicating this book for peace and happiness
in the world and to the loving hearts.

Acknowledgements

Deeply grateful to Amma who inspired, supported and made this book possible. Thanks to all my friends, especially Dev, Vinutha, Sudanand and Mamo for their kindness, thanks to my daughter, Sumera for the love and light and to my parents and brother for their care.

Foreword

It is the voice of the voiceless, the language of the soul.
Each one of them is written for someone, empathizing and
encouraging them to move ahead.

Anonymous

1. LET THERE BE

Let there be sweetness
Of the Air, Water and Plants
Of People, Animals and Birds
Let the minds be pure
Thoughts not clashing
All the souls connected
Through the thread of Love
Breathing the beauty of life!

2. BED OF ROSES

Trying to pluck the rose
She was pricked by the thorn
Her heart bled
Turning back, she saw

A bed of roses
Laid out for her
And she slept on it
Like a child in the womb
Of the Mother Earth
Caressed by her compassionate love

3. THE EARTH

With the moon as its flower
The ocean draping her
The Stars Shining around her
Brimming with life
The earth paints
A beautiful world
Burying all the pain
And hiding all the dirt
In its bosom

4. OPEN CAGE

She opened the door of the cage
The one inside her heart
Allowing her pet bird to fly
Freely without being bound
By the strings of her heart
She let the bird free
To explore the world
Waiting for it to return
Into her open cage
Whenever it wishes
To feed on her love

5. A PART

The tree gave me a part of it
I didn't realize how much
Pain passed through its nerves
Until I had to cut a part of me
To give to someone
I don't even know!

6. ONLY WHAT YOU LIKE

You want to hear only what you like
To feel only the nice things in life
But everything is packed
With both good and bad
You savour the good, endure the bad
The pain always makes the gain sweeter!
Tide over the bad with a smile
To have what you like
As you walk carrying the mixed bag of life!

7. SILENTLY

She chose to be silent
To hear His voice
She chose to be pure
With only His thoughts
Allowing herself be
A tool in His hands
Without altering
The beauty that He created

8. MUSIC

Like in a flute, the wind turns to music
Passing the seven notes, the chakras
The stomach like the accordion
Creating waves to pass through the hollow
The whole body becoming an instrument
Where you can play your own music

9. GEMS

You are like gems
That shine brightly
In many colours
Making the world
A beautiful place

Holding on to your
Presence, the support
The strength and the love
Thank you for making my life
A beautiful journey!!

10. LOOKING UP TO YOU

Looking up to You
For an answer
To know where to go
And what to do
I don't trust in me
But in You
Want to melt away
Every bit of me
So that You will
Fill me entirely
And lead me in the right way!

11. PART OF NATURE

Living in concrete buildings
Wearing gloves, boots and masks
Keeping away from the soil
Safely aloof from other creatures
Appreciating all man made things
Believing in only what is proven
To the worldly science
One can't but realise
That we are part of this Universe
One among all the creatures
The planets and all the stars
Our lives connected
With the marvel of the universe
No human mightier than nature
No science greater than universal truth.

12. FREE

Yours was a special life
Bound to your bed
Hidden from the world
You might have had lot of pain
Words that couldn't find voice
Feelings that couldn't find expression
And today as you bid farewell to this world
Hope your soul is finally rejoicing
To be able to fly freely
Not bound by the lamed body.

13. LIKE THE MOON

The moon that shines brightly
In the evening sky
Brighter as it draws closer to the Sun
Merely reflecting its light
So are we dark and empty
Without the light of the Divine
That we reflect
Shining brighter and brighter
As we get closer to the Light

14. THE COTTONY SEED

Like the cottony seed
With the delicate beard like covering
She held you in her hand
Gently without spoiling your plumage
Carrying the precious life
Blowing slowly without hurting you
She made you fly, fly into the beautiful world!

15. To the world above

Losing the grip from the hands that held you
You fall unprepared, fearfully, into darkness
Unaware of the depth and the danger
You let go of all that was held close to the heart
Your mind shuts its eyes, blind to the world
You start rising up, unaware, to the world above!

16. SHINING SOUL

The shining soul
That which you like to hold and own
In your greed to possess
You manifest, your nails grow sharp
Your eyes go blind
Heart ruthless and unkind
You tear apart the soul
And the heart bleeds

Let the soul be free and float happily
Reaching its destination with the love of the world!

17. BE READY TO FLY

Be ready to fly
Smoothing your wings
Choosing your target
Gaining all your strength
Steadying your mind
And as you fly high
I will watch you
Proudly, happily
While the tears wipe away all the pain!!

18. LETTING YOU GO

You might have come with a purpose
And I don't question you
I accept you with open hands
Accepting what god has offered
Whatever man might may say
I listen to His voice
Will hold you for a while
And let you go when you need to fly!!!

19. BUBBLES

The bubble in your hand
So lovely and colorful
A beautiful world
Filled with fantasies and joy
But don't be lost when it bursts
The bubbles are meant to be
Treasures of life not to be possessed
But to watch and let it go

Watch each bubble and enjoy
The world that brings with it!

20. WHO ARE YOU?

In the darkness under the drizzle
As the breeze brushed by
Sitting in the shadow of his image
In that silence, he asked:
Who are you?

I am nobody, my heart muttered
Searching each corner of my being
For an answer, I stared blankly
At his dark image that was ready
To laugh at my non-existence

My failure, my nothingness, my helplessness
The life that I lead into obscurity each day
Being nothing and nobody
Ignorant of the world and the life
Waiting anxiously for the final moment!

21. LIFE STARED BACK AT HER

She was walking together with life
Hand in hand step to step
Suddenly Life moved ahead
And looked back at her and stared
Asking her many questions
For which she had no answer

She stayed still, listening
To what life had to say
Her feet felt heavy
Unable to move,
She stared into eternity!

22. DIVINE LIGHT

All the Heart's desires
Melted away slowly
Leaving it blank
To reflect the divine light

23. WEANING OFF

Like lightning His hands worked
Weaning off all the heart's connections
To break free of worldly bondage
And get closer to Him

24. LIKE THE PLANETS

Like the planets that moved on their path
Tirelessly, undoubtedly
Like the sun rising and setting
Faithfully, unfailingly
Being part of the vast cosmos
They moved about
Fulfilling the duties of the world!

25. Moved with the Divine

Embraced by the universe
Comforted by unknown arms
Spoken to by the Cosmos
Heard by the space
Loved by the world
She moved with the divine

26. WORDS

Words, it is words again
That poured her feelings out
Into the space, into eternity
The silence absorbing the sound
And the pain!

27. TOWARDS DESTINY

Falling again into the pot holes of life
She lifted herself up
Looking at the vagaries of the illusory world
Longing yet loathing
The worldly ties that weaves a web of trap
Pulling you into its depths
Again and again
Forcing to move ahead steadily
Towards the destiny!

28. HARMONY

Like the still waters of a vast ocean
Like the darkness inside a long tunnel
Like a tune that is connecting the universe
The silence spoke of the harmony!

29. THE LAST FLOWER

That last flower has also fallen
The last smile fading
Free of the pain and the agony
That had passed through her
She walks leaving behind her facade
The world that was
Into the silence, the stillness
Where the flowers don't bloom, feelings aren't felt !

30. CAPTIVE !

The naive tender souls
With no malice in their hearts
Look terrified;
Terrified in the protective arms
of their tyrant protectors
Caged by the harsh rules
Unable to laugh their heart full
To play with their free will
The hands they extend
The pure hands which haven't seen
Not seen any discrimination
Are fearfully withdrawn
The angry looks that loomed
That loomed in front of them
Held them captive
Captive by the minds
That are older, meaner and cruel!

31. CAN THE TREE BE BLAMED?

Can the tree be blamed for not bearing the fruit
the bird likes
The wind, the sun, the moon and the earth
nurtured her
Nature made her bloom, with lovely flowers with
special fragrance
And soon luscious fruits appeared with her
unaware of it
The Bird darted towards her eager to savour them
in delight
Not the one it was looking for, the bird glared at the tree
loathing it
Unsure, the tree looked on, puzzled at the rage
of the bird
Can the tree blamed for not bearing the fruit
the bird wanted!

32. UNHEARD

The sound of bells ringing
Tickled her soul
The sight of birds in many hues
Made her heart smile
The flowers in full bloom
Kept her company
Beautiful melodies flowed in the air
And the knock at the door she longed for
Went unheard in her ears!

33. THE HEAT

The heat piercing through
Penetrating every inch of the body
Excruciating each cell

The unbearable pain
Manifesting itself
As dazzling golden flowers
In the height of summer
When the world is so cruel!

Thank you for the magnificent blooms
For showing
How the best of creations comes
From deepest of pain!

34. WHEN

It's when your soul burns like a wick
When everything inside you melts
When you forget your religion and yourself
That god enters you without looking for
Your name, your face nor your wealth!

35. RELISHED

Those unspoken words transformed into a beautiful song
Those tender feelings from the heart soaked her in love
Titillating music flowing around her led her to ecstasy
The flowers bloomed, the clouds changed their hue
The world filled with colours, smiles on all faces
She relished the moment she chose to share with herself!

36. SHOULD SHE

Should she laugh at the gimmicks of the world or allow to
be wounded
Bewildered by the ways of the world she stared at life
Where would she find solace
Nowhere but in the children of the world!

37. TILL YESTERDAY

Till yesterday you were an enemy
And today a friend
The flowers were in full bloom
And looked happy
Today when I looked out
They were gone
But they were in my neighbor's garden
Facing away from me
Till yesterday they were his enemy
An today they chose to be his friend!

38. IS THERE?

A silent witness to many a life's stories
A constant companion in the silent nights
As the lovers look at you from different zones
Telling you about those unspeakable pathos
I look at you with a barren heart
Is there anyone on the other side of the world waiting to
hear my story?

39. SHE SMILED

Amid the chaos, the familiar and the unfamiliar
The screams and the smiles and love and hurt
She walked, with a smile that bore signs of ecstasy
As million notes create music that breaks the wall
Which envelopes the world from eternity
She smiled and walked ahead into the universe!

40. REACHING OUT

She tried to reach out to
The one who smiled at her
She rushed to her with her pounding heart
To utter all the words that was
Taking life inside her, ready to be heard
Only as she reached very close to her
Did she know that she couldn't hear
Any words that the world uttered!

41. DESTINATION

She chose a clean path
Without any secret tunnels
The destination was far away
And too hard to reach
Whilst she saw a few
Who were making wily treads
She thought with her neat steps
She would be the chosen one
But at the end of the journey
She realised, that it is the destination
That really matters and not the treads
Though perhaps the divine would
Make an abode in clean and pure hearts!

42. Infinity

As she closed her eyes
She became part of infinity
The stars shone all around
All that she was, disappeared
Into this infinity, the divinity!

43. FIREFLIES

Fireflies twinkling
Heaven close to earth
The string of life
Swaying to the
Music of soul
In the silence
Of the dark still night
Their hearts spoke!

44. Do Not Ask

Do not ask me what I will do nor what I did
My yesterday I have lost it in memory
and tomorrow is not envisioned
Duties un-laid, suspended in the moment
I lay savoring the beauty, the pulse of the universe.

45. THE FUMES

Inside the glass bottle secured with a cork
The fumes moved about in its nascent form
And suddenly the seal was forced open
The fumes gushing out
Mixing with the particles in the space
Gaining new shades, and fragrance
In its new form, it felt being part of a bigger universe!

46. THE DIRT

The water might bring dirt too at times
To the shore,
But does the shore complain?
It always welcomes the sea
The waves of water that is its constant visitor!

47. NOTHINGNESS

From nothingness arises the absolute
When you surrender completely, you gain
What will an overfilled pot collect
Hold a pot with a drain
Which can receive all that is offered
Burn everything inside you and be just smoke
And dissolve into the vastness of the universe
In the stillness enfolding the secret of life!

48. OUR SALUTES

The path ahead of you is well laid out
It may be a lonely walk but no need to look back
We shall be watching you from behind
As you walk the distance, far away
Till you become one with the absolute
Our salutes and our greatest devotion
To you, our guiding light, our beloved!

49. THANK YOU

Thank you for cushioning my each fall
Why are you so kind to me
When i am not half as nice
As you want me to be!

50. Pierce Through

Like a baby coming out from the womb
She wanted to pierce through all the layers
And stand tall amidst the vastness
Facing the eternal sky,
With the strength of a warrior
And compassion of a mother!

51. THE FIERCEST

The most fiercest one might be guarding
A precious pearl deep within
Though not smiling at the world
But loving the ones near
The world might go unseen
The light inside the dark facade
The ones whose heart she touches
Never doubts her greatness!

52. MOTHER

Dear mother, don't ever leave me
You are my strength and my solace
Please forgive all my sinful acts
Lead me, let me follow your path
Let me not be allured by the worldly charms
But even if i do, will you forgive me
And still open your arms when i reach out for you??

53. SHE

Her gait was heavy and purposeful
Her each step, gently touching the earth
Without breaking the silence
The sweet smile on her face and the steady soft gaze
The world seemed rooted in her tresses
What shall I call her, the beautiful vision in front of me
Goddess of course, nothing less!

54. LET HER DANCE

Give the freedom for the heart to dance
It doesn't know any language nor any rules
Allow her to dance the way she wants
Freely, without any barriers
To the joy of life, the existence,
Let her dance to the glory of life!

55. YOUR DANCE

Please begin your dance and en-swathe me in it
Let the energy of the universe flow
Creating spectacular vibes of life, the Shakti
Want to move with the rhythm of your dance
Stepping on the world, crushing the evils under the feet
Tiding over the many waves and reach eternity!

56. Wild Flower

Apologies for being a wild flower
Not manicured nor cosmetic
She took the form that nature
Wanted her to be
Not to be presented
To the world as a piece of beauty
For the world to behold
But as part of the creation
To quietly add to the beauty of the world

57. LIKE TINY DROPLETS OF WATER

The love, the delight, the magic
All trapped in tiny droplets of water
Falling on the colocasia leaves
Which holds them in its palm
Without getting wet
And letting them roll out

Without leaving any mark on it!!

58. The Petals

The petals gets detached from the flower
And flies away in the gentle breeze
What was once a source of beauty
Now stands as a reflection of truth!

59. NEW SHEATH

Her skin started peeling away
All the tarnished ones
She had to get rid of them
To let new soft speckless ones
Cover her and give her a whole new feeling
Of purity and the kindness
Of the essence of life
May this new sheath never lose its shine!

60. THE OCEAN

The ocean seems silent, content with the world
but hidden in its depths are many stories
which it likes to say!

Hear, those who like to listen
The stories that come from the depths
Just a few moments together
To gain strength and to calmly face the world!

61. FINALLY

Finally the sea sees the shore
The mind sees the endless ocean of universal joy
All the worldly pain submerged under the deep ocean
She sat with the calm and quietness of the vast sea
With a smile that she hopes will never evade her face!

62. TRIAL

She faced the life's trial
Every bit of her existence questioned
She was accused, tormented
What was she to do
Erase herself form life's canvas
Or sketch herself anew?

63. MELTED

Like a candle
She melted as she burned
Suddenly losing her form
Which she had been all along.
Melted, she had become free
To create another form of herself
Which she could create
Without the past imperfections!

64. Move on

The feeling of being left out
Seeing the world go past
Your words go unheard
Tempted, you use the words
That people like to hear
To make them feel good
They will stop by
And take you with them
Though your feet may move with them
You know your heart remain where it stood!

65. How it Feels

Wish u understand how it feels
When world seems to shatter
And you don't have anything to hold on to
Spiralling down to the depths
As darkness looms over you
Your voice too weak to be heard
Unable to stretch the arms
You fall, completely betrayed, failed
Will there be light at the end of the tunnel?
You don't bother to know!

66. COLD

She lost her voice and with it her inner feelings
There was nothing that she wanted to share with the world
As she started viewing things the way it has to be
Floating like a piece of ice on an almost frozen lake
She became part of a larger canvas of life
All sensibilities having gone numb with cold
Freeing the mind from all earthly links

Life changed her beyond recognition!

67. THE TREE

As another flower withered and fell to the ground
Severing the deep bond they shared
The tree watched in silence, unable to feel any emotion
It was happy when it had fresh blooms
It looked bright and lovely, and everyone loved to see
But one by one it would all wither away
And drop to the ground, with beauty lost and no beholders.
The tree bore the pain of the cylce of life
All alone unable to shed any tears!

68. Caring Arms

Came into the world with a loud cry
But soon learnt to smile
Life looked bright and nice
Cuddled up in mamma's caring arms

So many people moving here and there
Pausing to give a nice warm smile
Life looked bright and nice
Cuddled up in mamma's caring arms

The world got bigger as i began to grow
Saw more shades that were bright and grey
But there was no moment to ponder
As life lead on with all its force

Too many hues and too many images
Not always all that pleasant
The bright, piercing blinding lights
Forcing my feet off the ground

The fear the uncertainty and the void
Made me search for those caring arms
That gave me warmth when i just arrived!

69. WHEN

When the world became too little
Rose the feeling to rise above
Breaking the bond from the ground
Floating among the clouds
Fully enamoured by one's own vision
Blind to the innocence and pain
Of the kind, loving souls!

70. IT RAINED LAST NIGHT!

Last night it rained
The earth quivered
As the tiny droplets
Fell on it as though
They were caressing her
Loving her and assuring
Of the beauty of life
The earth bloomed
As new Life sprouted
Bringing in new colours
And new fragrances
She revelled in joy
But soon the rain drops turned red
The world turned a battleground
With bloodshed all around
And beauty lost, happiness unfound
She looked on with deep unbearable pain
Tear drops and blood making her quiver again!

71. THE SHOW GOT OVER!

The show got over and everything came to a standstill
The seats were empty without the animated faces
That filled the hall until a while ago
The bright lights that lit up the evening were turned off
Darkness loomed all over, as he groped in the dark
Aimlessly with an empty but heavy heart

The stage that was brimming with great energy
As the artist moved vibrantly, creating
Celestial images to the soulful music;
The divine melody that reverberated all around
Is now abruptly shrouded by silence and darkness
As though life has just been snatched away

He was happy and had people all around him
But now he was left all alone, not knowing
Where to go nor what to do; His heart empty but heavy!

72. EVERLASTING BLISS!

When even the butterflies cheat
What's there in the world to look for
But wait for the end of the road
Whereby you will be liberated into
A whole new world of everlasting bliss!!

73. NOT AFRAID!

In the silence the words were clear
In the darkness the image was near
The voice that came straight from the heart
The vision that captivates you like art
Like an ocean that's calm and wide
The men who have cut their chords fine
Not afraid of the solitude, darkness and quiet!

74. DEFEAT

She might have lost the battle
But she deserves an olive crown
For her faith and her love for life!
The winner might get all the glory
But hers is a story of survival
Which the fainthearted could read!

75. MIRROR

Delving deep, she discovered
That there is nothing
Which she could call her own
The world, the feelings, the people
All were nothing but an illusion
A reflection of the temporary life

As the world unfolded infront of her
She reflected the vivid images
Like a gleaming mirror
Without any image or song of its own
There was nothing in the world
That she could change or possess!

76. WORDS OF BURDEN

They were just words
The only things that she had
It told her story
Of how she felt within
Love, longing, joy and pain
And all that her heart knew

While the world longs for some love
She gave away all that she had
Words of love, longing, joy and pain
Said without any restrain
Life burdened by her words
He begged to be left alone!

77. MARCH AHEAD

Something doesn't seem to be right
You can't put yourself behind
Nothing else should matter but you
For you need to lead on your own
Pulling thyself of all the troubles

There is no need to hesitate
Nobody is going to stay
March ahead, you will feel stronger
You will see the light in the end
Destiny waiting for you with open arms!

78. INNER VOICE

There was a voice that I could hear
Coming from nowhere and trying to say
Something that I didn't want to hear

I carried on without caring
And took that hasty step
Despite the warning that I heard

Yet again the damage was done
Misery brought about by an hasty act
Wish as always in the end
That I heeded to my Inner Voice!

79. A LOTUS BLOOMED

The mind fought to conquer the deadly serpent
A manifestation of the selfish love
Emanating from the seat of evil

Struggling to win over the growing serpent
The mind closed its eye and gained strength
And overpowered the vicious creature
As a thousand petal lotus bloomed!

80. THE SPITEFUL LOVE

You can't blame me now, she said
As she had asked him to kill
The spiteful creature wound around his neck
Slowly choking and leading him to death

She gave it life
Thinking it would bear fruits of love
Not realising that it would turn into a deadly serpent
Leading to misery

It isn't too late, she said
He could free himself of the vicious creature
That has wound itself around him
And making him unable to move

Kill it, show no mercy
Love that hurts isn't true love
Kill it, show no mercy
She wants to be free of the spiteful love!

81. An ode to a sweet soul

An ode to the sweet soul
Who flew to the land where her roots are

Like a butterfly with tender wings
She amused the curious eyes with her unique beauty

Colourful she was and had lot of stories to tell
Which she did guarding herself from the prying eyes

The dance of the land lured her
Dwelling deep, her body created beautiful images

The divine movements
Creating a stream of visuals connecting you to the world
above

She found a new voice to tell her stories
Through the mesmerizing art that overflowed in her heart

Her stories reached far and wide
Spreading the dance of the hinterland that allured her

But would anyone see her as the little butterfly she is
Who once stole the heart of a curious onlooker?

82. BEST EMOTION!

He said to nurture Love
No other feeling is worth knowing

Realise the feeling inside you
And share it abundantly

Don't ponder over other emotions
As love is the best to feel and to give!

83. HE BECAME A YOGI!

The world was unfair to him
His mind was filled with anger
And heart full of sadness

God had made him special
He was not an ordinary soul,
Who could be easily understood

He wanted the world to be fair
And fought all that was unjust
Making people move away from him

As loneliness became his companion
He realised the world was nothing
But a thin delicate bubble

Walking away from this momentary world
Leaving all his desires behind
He became a Yogi!

84. When I Go to Heaven

When I go to heaven I shall shower you
With flowers of sweet fragrance

As it fall all around you
Your life shall reflect its beauty

I would remove all the hurdles from your path
And fill it with red roses

I shall wipe away all your tears
And fear shall no more be with you

The world will see your beautiful heart
And would smile back at you

There shall be happiness all around you
As you will be blessed with everything nice!

85. NEW MUSIC

There is music flowing
From a distant far

It finds its way into my heart
And engulfs it with joy

I dance to the new music
With my body and soul

There is magic in the air
As i romanticize with the new melody

My heart overflows with a new found love
I want to dance to this music till my feet fail

Let this music never stop to reach me
Granting thus the happiness that I always sought!

86. I REJOICE

Like a whiff of fresh fragrance
In the cool gentle breeze
You came and made me relish
The beautiful feeling

As you awaken my heart and soul
And soothe them with lovely words
That comes straight from your heart;
I rejoice!

87. FIGHT

She fought without realising
That she already lost the battle

There are some things in life
Which you can't fight for

God knowingly gives you
Things that you dearly need

Sometimes when you lose
Don't have to feel heartbroken

Since He will bring you
Things that you dearly need!

88. TRUSTING IN YOU

Is He testing me always
By throwing hurdles at me?

Is He trying to come closer
By taking people far from me?

He taught me about people
How easily they change colour!

It is only in Him I can trust
Who pulls me up each time I fall

He is my strength, my saviour
And He has blessed me abundantly

I thank Him for his unconditional love,
For showing the light and the way

And bringing blessed people close to me;
Without whom it wouldn't have been easy!

89. A NEW WORLD

Wipe out the tears
Wash away the pain

Bring in some love
Ring in a new dawn

Let there be no blood shed
No hatred or vengeance

Light the minds of those in the dark
Who wage war for no real reason

Let not the innocents pay the price
For ignorant crimes of the few

Flood the world with beauty
Kindness and strength

Let us care for our world, our people
Share with our fellow beings

And create a better world
For the new tender souls!

90. DESIRE

It was after much despair
That I came to realize
How better life is
Without the word desire

Desire which made me whine
For want of things far beyond
There was no need to seek them
When all I wanted was happiness
That was just a few steps away!

91. THE ENDLESS SEARCH

As she searched for the answers she realized
That she has been moving in circles all the while

There would be no end to the search
No answers to the myriad questions

That was the truth and as she turned back
Life welcomed her back with open arms

And she decided to live, to live every moment!!

92. LOVE

My guard slipped off and her words pierced me like sharp arrows
Draining my heart of love and beauty
There was no glow on my face anymore as a frown replaced it
Why this unhappiness, hurt and insecurity?
These aren't the feelings that I want to nurture within
I fell again but managed to rise as I let love and beauty back
This is the wonderful world I want, filled with love and beauty
I put my guard back right in place not to let love drain out again!!!

93. The Choice

Through the narrow winding roads she walked
Overcoming the countless obstacles

Stumbling and struggling, she took newer steps
Until she came to the cross roads

It was time to make decisions, to make choices
Which she had to take on her own

She looked around, broadening her view
World became clearer, as she got an overview of things

There were two paths right in front of her
She could choose either, it was her choice

It was her choice indeed, she only needed to see
And choose which path to take

The path of happiness or the path of sorrow!!!!

94. BATTLE OF LIFE!

Like warriors they marched
Their bodies wounded and bleeding
Fighting with all their might
They couldn't quit the battle
The battle of life!

95. PETTY SENTIMENTS AND TEARS

Petty sentiments and persistent tears have no meaning
These words were stamped on my heart
Its weight made me feel very heavy
And I collapsed, I was speechless
I looked up, the world stared at me in silence

Why was I so petty and why did I shed those tears?
It's only love and joy that people like to share
Not petty sentiments about the world around
It's not your tears that people want from you
But its laughter and pleasure that they seek

Keep thy feelings for the world to thyself
Shed tears only in the dark and in the rain
Nobody understands thy better than thyself
We are our best friends and let us love ourselves!

96. A FLOWER

It was a pleasant summer morning
She stood under the tree which had lovely lavender blooms

Suddenly a wind blew
And the flowers fell on her like a shower of blessing

She felt very blessed as she enjoyed the wonderful feel
And sat down and gently picked one flower from the ground

The flower she preserved and stayed with her for long
It was a treasure, time captured in those tender petals

A token to look back and enjoy the beautiful moment!

97. THE DRY LEAF

The leaf was dry
It knew life was nearing the end

The corners of it started curling up
There was nothing for it to look for in the world

The world around it was dry
There were no rains, no river, nor any lake

But out of the blue, a kind soul came
And showered it with a pot full of water

The leaf looked out in bewilderment
It couldn't believe what was happening

The leaf suddenly straightened up
The dried parts came alive, it became green

It was a pretty picture
With tiny droplets of water resting on it

The breeze saying sweet nothings
And brushing gently against it and making it sway along

The world looked brighter
All straightened up it looked around eagerly

Enjoying the world around
It thanked the kind soul who brought Life back

98. SOAKED IN HIS LOVE

Soaked in his love, she walks through the deserted moonlit street
It's raining and you hear the thunder as the lightning strikes
Almost naked, she tries to cover herself
The wind is chilly and the rain drops pierce through her body
She tries to walk, dragging her feet
The rain is heavy and she is completely drenched;
Fully soaked in his love
She drags herself to the other end of the road for shelter!

99. CHANGE

The world looks brighter
I could see smiling faces all around
They were kind and friendly
And made me feel good
It was not very long back
That these faces had a frown
And weren't too kind
But they had changed, and it made me happy
I looked again and found that they were the same
It didn't take me long to realize
That it was me who had changed!!

100. HE

The day was bright and pleasant
There was laughter and happiness

Suddenly my world shook
And there was fury

I was in the abyss again
All alone in the dark

I looked for some known faces
But there were none

I was all alone in the darkest of the darkness
And I looked up to Him for help

He was there for me as always
He scooped me in his arms and brought me up yet again!

101. THANK YOU

There's a new dawn, a new song
A cool gentle breeze caressing the face

There's a new joy and laughter
A whole new world that i belong

There's a new strength, a greater resolve
A helping hand waiting to take you ashore

There's a new light and new way
A sweet tender smile straight from the soul

There's beauty all around, it's lovely
A heart filled with happiness and love

There's no escape, nowhere to hide
And here's a thank you for making me feel the way i do.